DR. MARTIN LUTHER KING, JR.
(COLOR AND LEARN)

An Illustrated History Coloring Book For Everyone!

If you like the book, please leave a review on wherever you bought and share your beautiful colored designs with the world.

ISBN: 978-1-64845-059-4

GET OUR NEW BOOKS!

Sign up to our VIP Newsletter to not miss our new book releases and to take part of **free book giveaways** and so much more!

www.ColorAndLearn.com/free

CONTENTS

INTRODUCTION

When people think of the civil rights movement and the fight for the rights of African Americans in the United States, the first name that comes to mind is Martin Luther King, Jr. This is a man who devoted his life to shining light on the inequalities and indignities that African Americans suffered daily. He went on to organize protests and strikes that changed the laws and even changed the U.S. Constitution.

Martin Luther King, Jr. worked as a civil rights activist during the 1950s and 1960s. He believed that the color of a person's skin should not decide their destiny and that the laws that said otherwise needed to be changed. Because of his beliefs his house was bombed, his family's life was put at risk, and he was eventually assassinated, all because of his fight to correct the wrongs that he could not ignore.

His ideas about how to fight these inequalities between whites and blacks came from his deep roots in the African American Baptist Church and from the teachings of Indian leader, Mahatma Gandhi, who believed in fighting oppression peacefully by using nonviolent protest or civil disobedience.

In 1955, Martin Luther King, Jr. led the first major successful protest by African Americans in the civil rights movement. It was known as The Montgomery Bus Boycott and protested the fact that blacks were forced to sit only at the back of the public bus while the seats at the front were reserved for whites. The protest included boycotting or not using the bus at all.

The 381-day bus boycott led to the United States Supreme Court ruling on December 20th, 1956, which declared such practices were against the Constitution of the United States. It was an especially important victory for the civil rights movement. King went on to organize and lead many more successful marches and campaigns that changed the laws so that all Americans, no matter their color, had the same rights.

In 1964, King received the Nobel Peace Prize for his work. He was 35 years old, and at the time he was the youngest person ever to receive the Peace Prize. King has been honored in numerous ways for his leadership and work. In the United States, each year the third Monday in January is a national holiday. It is called Martin Luther King, Jr Day in honor of this great man.

Let's learn more about this amazing man and what he accomplished in the name of freedom and equality.

EARLY LIFE

Martin Luther King, Jr. was born on January 15th, 1929 in Atlanta, Georgia in the Southern part of the United States. His parents were both college educated and the family lived a stable, middle class life. He grew up in a loving home with his extended family in a house his grandfather bought for $3,500.

The family home was on a street called Auburn Avenue in a part of Atlanta they called the *"Black Wall Street,"* since so many successful Black-owned businesses were located there. There were many role models within King's family and his neighborhood. This allowed him to see that African Americans could be just as successful as all other Americans if given a chance and if the discrimination that they faced was removed.

King's father was a minister in a well-respected African American Baptist church in Atlanta. It was called Ebenezer Baptist Church, and his grandfather, his mother's father, Reverend Adam Daniel Williams, had also been the pastor at Ebenezer from 1914-1931.

Both his father and his grandfather believed in improving the lives of their people and were members of the National Association for the Advancement of Colored People (NAACP) which was the most important national civil rights organization at the time. Observing his father and grandfather from an incredibly young age helped sow the seeds for King's later work.

King was originally given the name Michael King, but when he was five years old his father changed his son's name to Martin Luther King, Jr. He did this in honor of the 16th century German religious leader and reformer, Martin Luther.

Although the young King grew up in a happy, vibrant, and engaged family, he was not safe from the racial prejudice of the time. Atlanta is in the southern part of the United States and at the time whites and blacks were kept apart from each other by a policy called segregation. There were churches for whites and others for blacks. The same applied to schools, hotels, public transport, parks, and restaurants; in fact, it was the law.

When King was six years old, one of his friends told him that they could no longer play together. The young boy was white. The boy's mother told him that since King would be going to a school that only allowed African American children, and this boy would be going to a whites-only school, they should no longer be friends. This sort of discrimination was common in the lives of African Americans and even at that young age King knew it was wrong.

SLAVERY

Unlike other Americans, African Americans did not originally come to America willingly. Instead, they were stolen from their homes throughout Africa, forced onto ships and brought across the sea to North America. The ships took them further on to America where they were sold to white people, who forced them to work in their homes and on their farms for no pay. They were kept as slaves and treated brutally. They were sold as if they were not human beings but rather objects to be owned. Often, even mothers were separated from their children with no mercy shown to anyone.

Slavery had been legal in America since its colonial days, which began in the 1500s. It wasn't until 1865 that the Thirteenth Amendment to the U.S. Constitution made it illegal. The American Civil War, which went from 1861 to 1865, was fought over the issue of slavery. The Union, made mostly of the northern states, wanted slavery to stop and be abolished forever, however the Confederate States, primarily from the south, wanted slavery to continue. A brutal civil war was fought that divided the nation.

On January 1st, 1863, President Abraham Lincoln issued the Emancipation Proclamation that freed all slaves. Since the war was still being fought, the Confederate States did not recognize the proclamation; they didn't even recognize President Lincoln as their president. When the war finally ended in June 1865, all slaves in America, including in the Southern states, were finally free.

Once the slaves were free, they could now marry legally, own their own homes, and get an education. The brutality of slavery, including whippings and the separation of families by selling people, was a thing of the past. However, life was still very hard. During the time that people had been slaves, they had earned no wages and had not been allowed to receive any education. When they were suddenly freed, they had neither land nor other resources to begin to build a life. Most were desperately poor and had to accept unfair contracts with their former owners.

Many became sharecroppers. In sharecropper arrangements the former slave would rent a piece of land from the white landowner. When the crop was ready for harvest, a percentage of the crop was paid back as rent to the former slave owner. Although the former slaves had freedom, life was still extremely hard, and most lived in poverty. This would be the case for many generations to come, all because of the legacy of how they arrived in America.

DID YOU KNOW?

- The total number of Africans brought to the United States during the time that slavery was legal was 472,381.

- In total, 12 million Africans were kidnapped on the continent and sold into slavery around the world.

- 620,000 American soldiers died in the American Civil War, more than any other war the United States has fought. The death toll from World War I for Americans, for example, was 116,516 and World War II was 405,399.

- The bloodiest battle during the Civil War was the Battle of Gettysburg, Pennsylvania, which was fought in 1863 from July 1st to July 3rd. The result was 51,000 dead and wounded by the time the fighting ended.

- During the Civil War, a Union soldier, if he was white, received $13 per month as a wage. A black Union soldier received $7 per month. In 1864, this difference in pay was sorted out so that they both received the same amount.

- The Southern states did not secede (separate) from the union, declaring themselves no longer a part of the United States all at one time. They declared their independence one at a time. For example, the first state to secede was South Carolina on December 20th, 1860. The last state to secede was Tennessee on June 8th, 1861.

JIM CROW LAWS

To understand the mountain Martin Luther King, Jr. was about to climb when he set out to change the lives of African Americans, you need to understand how the Africans arrived in the United States through the brutal institution of slavery. The other important factor is the laws that were then put in place to keep blacks below whites. These laws were called Jim Crow laws.

Immediately after the 13th Amendment and the end of the Civil War, white people, especially the ones in the Southern United States, wanted to still control their former slaves. They created The Black Code, which was a series of state and local, and city and county laws that defined where former slaves could work, how they could work, and how they should be paid. The Black Code, for all practical purposes, kept slavery in place but labelled it with a different word.

The Black Code was expanded and eventually became known as the Jim Crow laws. These laws existed from after the Civil War until 1964 when President Lyndon B. Johnson signed The Civil Rights Act, ending all Jim Crow laws.

Jim Crow laws were about legalizing racial segregation or separation, where facilities, opportunities, services, and many other public places were organized according to which race you were. For example, certain public toilets had signs that stated they were only for African Americans, usually called *"Colored,"* while others were for whites only. Supporters of segregation often liked to say that the facilities were *"separate but equal,"* but that was never the case. The facilities for blacks were always inferior and usually significantly so.

Jim Crow laws were common in the South, although they were also found in the North. There were White only neighborhoods and in theaters, and there were different entrances and seats for blacks and whites. There were black schools and white schools, black public pools, and white ones. Some restaurants had signs reading *"Whites Only"* and even some towns made it clear when entering that African Americans were not allowed. These laws made marriage between blacks and whites illegal and often made voting for African Americans difficult. The rule would be that a person must own property to register to vote, knowing full well that few African Americans owned property because of the legacy of slavery.

Blacks who tried to fight Jim Crow laws were arrested, fined, often jailed, and sometimes even killed. During the era of Jim Crow, a racist vigilante group grew in numbers and were known as the Klu Klux Klan (KKK). People in this group, which is still in existence, wore white robes and white hoods that covered their faces. They terrorized and sometimes even killed any African American who attempted to fight Jim Crow laws.

MARTIN GROWS UP

As a child, Martin Luther King, Jr. attended segregated black schools in Atlanta. He was a good student and skipped two years of high school, graduating from Booker T. Washington High School at the age of fifteen.

In 1944, he was accepted into Morehouse College in Atlanta through a special program for gifted students. The summer before heading off to college, King took a job on a tobacco farm in Connecticut. That experience opened his eyes to a new way of seeing the world.

Having lived his entire life up until then in the South, going to a northern state like Connecticut, was a huge learning experience. There he saw that blacks and whites could work, play, and worship together. The Jim Crow laws didn't exist, so he could go to the movies or a restaurant freely. He understood even more that race was not an issue to separate people and his hatred for segregation grew. In a letter to his parents that summer, he wrote about how he was surprised to go to church with white people and to be able to enter any restaurant that he wanted.

He returned to Atlanta and began his university education. At Morehouse, he was deeply influenced by the college's president, Benjamin Mays, an inspirational academic who had a commitment to civil rights. Mays is sometimes considered King's intellectual father. Mays gave the eulogy speech at King's funeral, a speech now referred to as, *"No Man is Ahead of His Time Speech."* In it he said:

> *"If Jesus was called to preach the Gospel to the poor, <u>Martin Luther</u> was called to give dignity to the common man. If a prophet is one who interprets in clear and intelligible language the will of God, Martin Luther King, Jr. fits that designation. If a prophet is one who does not seek popular causes to espouse, but rather the causes he thinks are right, Martin Luther qualified on that score."*

At first, when he arrived at Morehouse, King considered studying law or medicine, but by his last year he settled on following in his father's and grandfather's footsteps and joining the ministry. He entered Crozer Theological Seminary in Chester, Pennsylvania and was ordained as a Baptist minister on February 25th, 1948. He was nineteen years old.

After Crozer, in 1951, King was accepted at Boston University for graduate studies. In June of 1955, he received a Doctorate of Philosophy degree in Systematic Theology.

GANDHI AND NONVIOLENCE
CIVIL DISOBEDIENCE

At Morehouse College, King discovered Mahatma Gandhi and his ideas about how to fight unjust laws using civil disobedience. This discovery changed the way King approached the fight for the rights of black people and became a policy for all of the protests he was involved in.

Gandhi was born in India in October 1869. He was a Hindu from Gujarat in Western India. Gandhi studied law in the United Kingdom but upon his return to India, he struggled to keep a practice going. He took what was meant to be a short trip to South Africa in 1893 to represent an Indian businessman who lived there. He ended up staying in South Africa for twenty-one years.

Finally, in 1915, at the age of forty-five Gandhi returned to India. By this time, the British had colonized India and treated the native Indians as second-class citizens in their own country. Gandhi found it awfully hard to accept the situation. He soon began to organize various protests. The first was in response to exceedingly high land taxes and the next was a call for the British to leave India.

Soon Gandhi became the leader of the Indian National Congress and his fight for self-rule became stronger. He also led protests for women's rights, pushed for the various religions in India to get along, and for help for the poor. Most protests, however, were about his desire for the British to leave India.

Gandhi called his method of protest *"non-cooperation."* He believed that the reason the British were able to control the people and the country was because the Indian people cooperated. If the Indians stopped cooperating, the British would be forced to leave. Eventually, in August of 1947, the British did leave and left India to govern itself.

This sort of non-cooperation is called nonviolent civil disobedience. It is when a person actively chooses to disobey a law. For example, protestors might decide that a restaurant that would not serve African Americans should be filled up by a large group of African Americans. Perhaps they would just go inside and sit down quietly. They would not damage anything and would not be violent in any way, even when violence was used on them.

King found this idea intriguing. He knew from a young age that segregation and the Jim Crow laws were wrong. After learning about Mahatma Gandhi's non-violent approach, he knew this was the right way to bring the hated Jim Crow laws to an end.

MARRIAGE AND FAMILY

While in Boston at college, King met Coretta Scott. Coretta was from Alabama and was studying music at The New England Conservatory of Music on a scholarship. She was an accomplished musician, playing both piano and trumpet and singing soprano.

Coretta was from Marion, Alabama and the third child of four. She was born in her parent's house and delivered by her great grandmother who had been a former slave.

Even before she met King, Coretta was active in the civil rights movement. She was a member of the National Association for the Advancement of Colored People (NAACP).

She graduated as valedictorian of her high school class and went to Antioch College in Yellow Springs Ohio before winning the scholarship to the music conservatory in Boston.

A friend gave King Coretta's telephone number, but when he called her to ask her out on a date she nearly refused. When they did go on their first date, Coretta was surprised at how short King was. He, on the other hand, told her that first evening that she had all of the qualities that he wanted in a wife. She told him he couldn't know that, since they'd only just met. Despite the rocky start, they started dating regularly, and after two weeks King told his mother that he had met his wife.

Things were not smooth sailing though, because Kings' father, Martin Luther King, Sr. was not impressed with Coretta when he first met her. He told her that he didn't approve of the sort of music that she made and that his son had high prospects and was in much demand. Coretta responded saying that she too had high prospects.

Still, they were married on June 18th, 1953 at Coretta's mother's house. Martin Luther King, Sr. married the couple.

The newlywed couple stayed in Boston until King completed his thesis for his doctorate degree. Then he got a job as a pastor at Dexter Avenue Baptist Church in Montgomery, Alabama. That move proved important, because in Montgomery, King would enter the national stage as a leader in the civil rights movement.

The couple went on to have four children: Yolanda, Martin III, Dexter, and Bernice.

ROSA PARKS

When King and his wife moved to Montgomery in September 1954, Rosa Parks was already an active member of the Montgomery Branch of the NAACP. Little did King know how her actions would push him to the front of the civil rights movement.

Rosa Parks was born in 1914. She was raised by her mother on her mother's parents' farm in Pine Level Alabama. Both of her grandparents had been former slaves and were strong supporters for the rights of African Americans. Parks remembered how her grandfather stood in front of their house with his shotgun while the KKK marched down their road.

Parks was forced to leave school at eleven when both her mother and grandmother became ill and she needed to take care of them. Later, though, with the help of her husband Raymond Parks, she finished her high school degree in 1933.

When she married Raymond in 1932, he was already an active member of the NAACP. He encouraged Rosa to be active in the organization too. She became the chapter's youth leader and then the secretary to the president of the Montgomery chapter.

On December 1st, 1955, Rosa was coming home from a long day of work as a seamstress at a department store. She got on the Cleveland Avenue bus to go home. At the time, Jim Crow laws were in full swing and black bus riders were made to sit at the back, while white riders were at the front. There was a sign in the middle, separating the two races. The laws were enforced so stringently that African Americans had to pay the fare at the front door, get off the bus and enter the bus through the back door.

On this particular day, there were many white passengers, such that some were standing. The bus driver noticed this, so he stopped the bus and moved the sign separating the white area from the black. Then he asked the four black passengers sitting in the front rows of the black section to move. Three stood up and moved, the fourth, Rosa, refused. She said she'd had enough of giving in.

The bus driver called the police and Rosa was arrested. She was put in jail and released on bail later that evening.

Rosa's court date was on December 5th and five hundred of her supporters packed the courtroom. The president of the NAACP told African Americans not to use the buses that day as a protest of Rosa's arrest. Rosa was fined $10 and $4 for the court fee.

Rosa's act of civil disobedience sparked the beginning of the civil right movement.

DID YOU KNOW?

- Mahatma Gandhi was arrested and imprisoned many times. In South Africa, he was arrested six times and another six times in India.

- Coretta Scott King's older sister, Edythe, was the first African American student of Antioch College. The school wanted to increase the number of black students in an attempt to diversify the student body. Coretta went there for a short time too.

- The Klu Klux Klan started as a private club, created by former Confederate soldiers in Pulaski, Tennessee in 1865.

- A U.S. Supreme Court ruling in 1954 in a case called Brown vs the Board of Education ended segregated schooling in the country. The court voted 9-0, stating that segregated schools were unconstitutional.

- Martin Luther King, Jr. believed that his own family should live a simple life because the movement required his time and money. The family only bought their first house in 1965 for $10,000.

MONTGOMERY BUS BOYCOTT

Rosa Parks' arrest infuriated the African American community in Montgomery, Alabama. They were tired of the indignities of the Jim Crow laws and the segregation of the city's buses.

A civil rights group in the city, Women's Political Council (WPC), made up of black professional women had already attempted (in 1954) to get the city to improve the bus system for blacks, who made up 75% of the passengers. Mayor W.A. Gayle wasn't interested.

Before Rosa Parks, two young African American girls, 15-year-old Claudette Colvin and 18-year-old, Mary Louis Smith, also refused to give up their seats to white passengers. They were arrested and fined. But Rosa Parks' case was the last straw and it ignited the city. King would later comment that Rosa Parks was an upstanding member of the community, well-respected and already working hard for the rights of African Americans. She was the perfect person to spark the light under the fire that was to become the national civil right movement that would once and for all end the evil system of segregation.

The leader of the WPC, Jo Ann Robinson, called for a boycott of the buses by African Americans on the day of Rosa Parks' trial, December 5th, 1955. But the word was spreading slowly. Ministers in the black churches and other leaders in the African American community met on December 2nd at King's Dexter Avenue Baptist Church to discuss the December 5th bus boycott, and how to make sure that it was a success.

With the push of the black churches behind them, on the day of the trial 90% of Montgomery's black bus riding public stayed off the buses. It was a success.

On the evening after the trial, still jubilant over the success of the one-day boycott, leaders met and at that meeting the Montgomery Improvement Association (MIA) was formed with King elected as its leader. Later, Rosa Parks said that they chose Dr. King to head the MIA because he was new to Montgomery and had yet to make any enemies.

At that meeting it was decided that the bus boycott would be extended indefinitely until their demands were met. The original demands included: black bus drivers on routes that went through primarily black neighborhoods, courteous treatment of black passengers by bus drivers, first come seating, and stops at all corners in black neighborhoods just as was done in white neighborhoods. What was glaringly missing on their list of demands was the removal of the segregated seating.

Even with such mild demands, the city commissioners and the bus company refused to accept them.

A 381-DAY BUS BOYCOTT

The African Americans of Montgomery boycotted the city's buses and walked, rode bicycles, or took taxis to go to work or to do their daily errands. The city officials and racist supporters of segregation tried their best to stop the boycott.

On January 30th, 1956, Coretta Scott King was at her home in Montgomery with her new baby, Yolanda, and a friend when they heard a loud noise on the porch. Later, it was discovered that the house had been bombed. Luckily, no one was injured. At the same time, the house of ED Nixon, the former head of the NAACP, was also bombed.

When members of the MIA and supporters of the boycott heard of King's house being bombed with his wife and young daughter inside, they crowded angrily at the front of his house.

King told them that they could bomb his house, even kill him, but another person would rise up to take his place and continue the struggle.

The city ordered black taxi owners to stop transporting black boycotters. If they refused to obey the orders they would be arrested or fined. In response, the MIA organized a group of 300 cars to make a carpool. Stranded African Americans could get lifts from the carpool, paying ten cents, just like they did on the buses.

In February, in frustration at the peaceful protests, the city pulled out a law from 1921 that said it was illegal to organize acts to stop lawful business. They used that law to arrest more than ninety leaders of the bus boycott, including King. He was tried, convicted, and ordered to pay $500 or serve 386 days in prison. The fine was eventually paid after an unsuccessful appeal, but the court case received national publicity and the boycott gained country-wide support. The city's efforts had back-fired spectacularly.

About the boycott, King said, *"We came to see that, in the long run, it is more honorable to walk in dignity than ride in humiliation. So … we decided to substitute tired feet for tired souls and walk the streets of Montgomery."*

By this time, complete desegregation of the buses was on MIA's list of demands. They took their case to the Montgomery's Federal Court, which ruled that bus segregation in the city violated the 14th Amendment of the Constitution. The amendment said that all citizens, regardless of race, are guaranteed equal rights and protection under state and federal law. The city appealed the ruling to the U.S. Supreme Court. On December 20th, 1956, the Supreme Court upheld the ruling and ordered Montgomery to desegregate its buses. On December 21st, the boycott ended. It lasted 381 days.

THE AFTER EFFECTS OF THE MONTGOMERY BUS BOYCOTT

There was reluctance on the part of the city, the bus company, and racist residents to accept the U.S. Supreme Court ruling. This resistance included violence.

Buses were shot at by snipers, and in one incident a pregnant black woman was shot in both of her legs. In the early hours of January 9th, 1957, dynamite blasts occurred around the city in six locations. Alabama Governor James E. Folson said that it was the work of anarchists wanting to stop bus segregation.

Three black churches were among the targets of the blasts: Mount Olive Baptist Church, Bell Street Baptist Church, and the home of a white minister of one of the black Lutheran churches, Reverend Robert Graetz. Also targeted that night were the homes of boycott leaders, Reverend Ralph D. Abernathy and King; although the dynamite at King's house was found before it could explode.

Bus services in the city were stopped and the governor offered a $2,000 reward for the capture of the bombers. On January 30th, 1957, seven bombers were arrested. All of them were members of the Klu Klux Klan. After this, the bus violence ended.

The successful Montgomery Bus Boycott was the first mass protest in the civil rights movement and paved the way for more protests to end Jim Crow laws all over the country. The method of using nonviolent civil disobedience to fight these unjust laws became a norm after the protests in Montgomery. The combining of the practice of nonviolent civil disobedience, with the ethics of his Christian beliefs, were solidified for King too. He knew this was the most effective way to bring an end to Jim Crow laws.

The Bus Boycott pushed King to the front of the civil rights movement, and in the eyes of most, he was from that point considered its leader.

The national attention that King and the boycott received, promoted the call for the end of segregation. It became the focus of conversations throughout the country.

FIRST QUIZ TIME!

1. What is the name of the well-known church where Martin Luther King, Jr.'s father and grandfather were ministers?

   a. Olive Street Baptist Church
   b. Ebenezeer Baptist Church
   c. Dexter Avenue Baptist Church

2. For approximately how many years was slavery legal in the land that is now called the United States of America?

   a. 100 years
   b. 200 years
   c. 300 years

3. The practice where freed slaves rented land from white landowners and paid the rent in a percentage of their harvest was called _____.

   a. Sharecropping
   b. Farm sharing
   c. Field rentals

4. Where did Martin Luther King, Jr. receive his doctorate (PhD) degree?

   a. Crozer Theological Seminary
   b. Morehouse College
   c. Boston University

5. Why was Mahatma Gandhi so important to Martin Luther King, Jr.?

6. In which city did the important bus boycott that launched the nationwide fight against?

INTERESTING QUOTES

Darkness cannot drive out darkness; only light can do that. Hate cannot drive out hate; only love can do that.

Martin Luther King, Jr.

Each person must live their life as a model for others.

Rosa Parks

Earth provides enough to satisfy every man's needs, but not every man's greed.

Mahatma Gandhi

SOUTHERN CHRISTIAN
LEADERSHIP CONFERENCE (SCLC)

King knew how to use public attention and publicity effectively. It was clear that the Montgomery Bus Boycott had been a great success and he didn't want to lose that momentum. At the same time, another civil rights activist, Bayard Rustin, was working on an idea of having a more coordinated approach to fighting segregation, not only on public buses but everywhere.

King invited sixty black church ministers to Ebenezer Baptist Church to discuss the idea. Afterwards, they had a few more meetings and the Southern Christian Leadership Conference (SCLC) was established on January 10th, 1957.

SCLC acted as an umbrella body and was governed by an elected board, with King voted in as its first president. The motto of the SCLC was: *"Not one hair of one head of one person should be harmed," therefore* cementing their commitment to social change using nonviolent civil disobedience.

The main purpose of the group was to get all organizations in the South working on the civil rights of African Americans, in particular the end of segregation. They would work together under one organization, so that each one would know what the others were doing. They could also support each other in their efforts. Their approach was different from organizations such as the NAACP that created chapters around the country. The SCLC set up an office on Auburn Street in Atlanta and employed one staff member, Ella Baker, a staunch civil rights activist.

There was a lot of opposition to the establishment of the SCLC, not only by white people but also by many blacks. Some Christians believed that social activism had no place in black churches, that church was for spiritual and charity needs and to help the poor and sick.

Because of the fierce opposition from racist white groups, such as the KKK and the White Citizens Council, many African Americans feared being associated in any way with SCLC. The opposition from these groups toward churches and organizations that associated with SCLC included: economic retaliation, such as the loss of jobs or loss of business for ministers and church leaders, violence, bombings, arson, and even death. Many African Americans were not willing to make those sorts of sacrifices.

There were also young African Americans who felt that the SCLC was not strong enough and that nonviolence was a weak strategy to oppose the evilness of segregation.

For King, the SCLC would be his vehicle for his war on segregation, as well as other issues such as poverty, that he soon realized worked hand-in-hand to keep blacks oppressed.

CITIZENSHIP SCHOOLS

One of the major projects of King's SCLC was the running of the Citizenship Education Program. Originally, this project was started by a group of people in Tennessee, the Highlander Folk School, who bought some land and set up a school to teach adult African Americans and the poor to read. The school was located in the middle of the Appalachian Mountains where many poor people lived, both black and white.

Teaching people to read may seem like a safe thing to do, but in the South at the time, the fact that a person could not read was a big problem. Many states had literacy tests that a person had to pass in order to register to vote. So, if you could not read, you could not vote, therefore, your rights were taken away. The Highland Folk School wanted to correct this and get more blacks exercising their right to vote.

The Tennessee government soon realized what the Highlander Folk School was up to. They took away their charter to run the school and eventually took even the land on which the school stood.

The SCLC saw the benefit of the Citizenship School and took up the project with most of the people from The Highlander Folk School remaining. They changed the name to the Citizenship Education Program.

The SCLC then opened a school in Dorchester Center in Midway, Georgia. Blacks from all over the South travelled to the school for the program. The SCLC also ran schools away from Georgia, in homes, churches, and community centers. The program was normally twelve weeks long with students coming for two hours, twice a week. The teachers in these schools were people who had finished the program in Dorchester Center. The objective of the program was to restore a first-class citizenship to people who had been denied one.

King, through the SCLC, taught blacks to read at the school, but they were also taught about democracy, about their civil rights, about community leadership, and practical politics as well as ways to resist unjust laws and policies. They were also taught how to recruit others to the cause. 69,000 teachers taught in the SCLC Citizenship Education Program, and between 1961 and 1968, 8,000 students went through the program.

PRAYER PILGRIMAGE FOR FREEDOM

On May 17ᵗʰ, 1957, 25,000 people gathered in the mall in Washington, D.C. in front of the Lincoln Memorial. They were there to commemorate the landmark Brown vs Board of Education decision by the Supreme Court that declared an end to segregated schools. The protest was called the Prayer Pilgrimage for Freedom. Martin Luther King, Jr. was billed as the last speaker of the day.

For King, it would be his first time speaking to a national audience. The gathering would also be marked as the largest civil rights protest up to that point.

It had been three years since the Supreme Court ruled that segregated schools were unconstitutional, but in the South, state and local governments were finding every way possible not to allow black children to go to school with white children. This was in direct violation to the ruling and the U.S. Constitution.

On February 14ᵗʰ, 1957, King and the SCLC sent a telegram to President Dwight D. Eisenhower asking him why he was unable to force the southern states to comply with the rule of law. In the telegram, King said that if Eisenhower could not maintain law and order, he would then have to lead his people to him so that he could better understand the organized terror African Americans faced in the southern states.

The organizers of the Prayer Pilgrimage had been asked by African American Congressman Adam Clayton Paul, Jr. not to embarrass Eisenhower, and the organizers largely agreed that they would not.

At the rally, King gave one of his famous speeches, titled *"Give Us the Ballot."* In it, he pushed for African Americans to be given their right to vote without any hindrance. He said that if African Americans could vote freely their problems would become a thing of the past.

He went through a list, each line starting with *"Give us the ballot and…"* It included lines such as *"Give us the ballot and we will no longer have to worry the federal government about our basic rights… Give us the ballot and we will no longer plead to the federal government for passage of an anti-lynching law."* The last line referred directly to the fact that Brown vs Board of Education was being largely ignored in the South and the Eisenhower administration was failing to do anything about it. He said, *"Give us the ballot and we will quietly and nonviolently, without rancor or bitterness, implement the Supreme Court's decision of May 17ᵗʰ, 1954."*

This speech put King firmly in the seat as the leader of the civil rights movement throughout the entire country.

STABBING IN HARLEM

On September 20th, 1958, Martin Luther King, Jr. was on a book tour, publicizing his book about the Montgomery Bus Boycott, *Stride Toward Freedom*, when he was nearly killed.

He was signing books at Blumstein's Department Store in Harlem, New York, when a middle-aged African American woman came up to the table. She asked him if he was Martin Luther King, Jr. and he replied that he was. The woman said that she had been looking for him for five years. She then took a steel letter opener out of her purse and stabbed King just at the bottom of his throat.

The police arrived and took the woman, Izola Curry, into custody. Curry, 42, was mentally ill. Later she was diagnosed with paranoid schizophrenia and spent the rest of her life in various mental hospitals.

King was sitting calmly on a chair when the police arrived. One officer warned him not to move or even sneeze, for fear the letter opener would move and stab his heart.

King was rushed to Harlem Hospital where surgeons opened his chest and removed the letter opener. One doctor commented that the police officer on the scene had given King particularly good advice. During the surgery, they saw that the blade of the letter opener was sitting on the aorta and with the wrong move could have easily killed King.

In a press conference on September 30th, King said that he held no ill-will for Mrs. Curry and hoped that she would receive the help that she needed. He also recommitted himself to the practice of nonviolent civil disobedience despite the violent attack.

KING'S TRIP TO INDIA

From February 5th to the 18th of March 1959, King, his wife Coretta, and another member of the MIA traveled to India to further understand the theory of nonviolent resistance and to learn more about King's personal guide in the practice of Mahatma Gandhi. According to King, Gandhi was *"the guiding light of our technique of nonviolent social change."*

The previous year, the prime minister of India, Pandi Jawaharlal Nehru, had visited the United States and showed interest in King visiting India. Unfortunately, previous engagements and the stabbing in Harlem had stopped King from being able to visit the country. After his doctors gave him the all clear, King decided it was time to tour India.

In his papers describing the trip, he said that everywhere they went people knew him and he was greeted with large enthusiastic crowds. The press in India had covered the Montgomery Bus Boycott religiously. He met Gandhi's family and they were happy that King had brought the idea of nonviolent resistance to a global stage with the boycott.

During the trip, King began to see that the oppression of people, especially people of color, was a global problem. He could see that the people of India, like the African Americans in the United States, had come far but still had a long way to go.

He had many interesting debates and discussions about using nonviolent resistance to face down oppression. Some people agreed with it, some did not. King also made sure that he visited the place where Mahatma Gandhi's ashes were entombed, laying a wreath in his honor.

When he returned to the United States, King was more committed than ever to the power of using nonviolent resistance to change the laws and attitudes that oppressed African Americans.

CIVIL RIGHTS ACT OF 1957

In 1957, only 20% of African Americans were registered to vote. In some voting districts in the southern states, blacks were the majority and racist whites feared that they might vote against them, so tried their best to keep African Americans from being able to vote. This was usually done by passing laws at state and local levels that put barriers up and stopped blacks from being able to register to vote. African Americans were being disenfranchised, meaning they were having their right to vote as citizens of the country taken away.

President Eisenhower and his attorney general, Herbert Brownell, decided to put together an act to protect the voting rights of African Americans. This was the Civil Rights Act of 1957. Although in Congress some of the key parts of the act were removed by congressmen from the South, the act did accomplish a few important acts including:

1. The establishment of a Civil Rights Department in the Justice Department.

2. It declared that the protection of voting rights was the duty of the government.

3. Allowed federal officials to prosecute cases where voting rights were being denied although the penalties were mild (fines not over $1,000 and six months in prison).

4. It created a six member U.S. Civil Rights Commission that was to investigate cases where voting rights were being denied.

Beyond these improvements, the passing of the act showed that the federal government had interest and commitment to civil rights.

Despite the good intentions of the act, by 1960 the number of black people registered to vote had only increased by 3%.

LUNCH COUNTER SIT-INS

By 1960, Martin Luther King, Jr. had moved his family to Atlanta to concentrate his efforts on the civil rights movement. He also became co-pastor of Ebenezer Baptist Church with his father.

At that time, many department stores in the South had lunch counters that were segregated; only whites could sit there. College students around the South decided to tackle this issue by doing sit-ins at these counters.

The first one took place on February 1st, 1960, at the Woolworth's lunch counter in Greensboro, North Carolina. Four African American students from A&T College bought some items and then sat down at the lunch counter. The waitress asked them to leave and the students politely told her that they would not. The police were not called, and no one was arrested. The students remained at the lunch counter until the store closed.

The next morning the students again sat at the lunch counter, although by then the group had grown to more than twenty. The newspapers of the area covered the act of resistance and soon the lunch counter sit-ins grew into a movement that was taken up by others in the South. By the end of February, sit-ins had taken place in thirty places located in seven states. 50,000 students participated in the sit-ins.

King later wrote, *"The key significance of the student movement lies in the fact that from its inception, everywhere, it has combined direct action with non-violence. This quality has given it the extraordinary power and discipline which every thinking person observes."*

In October of 1960, Atlanta students asked King to join their planned sit-in at Rich's department store in Atlanta. He joined them as a follower, not a leader, to support their cause. In this case, the police were called, and 280 students were arrested including King. They were kept in jail for between five and six days and released. King was released but then immediately re-arrested. The police and judge decided that his arrest at the lunch counter violated his parole for a previous traffic offence, which he was on parole for.

In his papers, King explained that as part of the general harassment that he lived with; the police had arrested him for driving in Georgia with an Alabama license. His lawyer had told King that it was dealt with. King hadn't realized that *"dealt with"* meant that the lawyer pleaded guilty and paid a fine. The court had then given King a six-month parole. That parole was what the sit-in arrest violated. Because of that King was sentenced to four months hard labor at Georgia State Prison.

HOW THE KENNEDYS HELPED
GET KING RELEASED

When King was arrested, he was taken to the local jail, but then in the early morning of October 26th, at about 3 a.m., they put him in a vehicle and drove him 280 miles to Georgia State Prison. They shackled his legs and tied him to the floor of the vehicle as if he had committed a profoundly serious crime. Civil rights activists were angry about the way King was treated.

At that time, John F. Kennedy was the Democratic nominee for U.S. president. Kennedy and King had met on two previous occasions, once when he was still a senator and again when he was nominated. At first, King was not impressed with Kennedy's stance or voting record on civil rights. By the time Kennedy became the Democratic nominee. King could see that he had educated himself about the daily plight of African Americans and he seemed to understand the issues better.

Kennedy had wanted King and the SCLC to invite him to speak to their members, but King refused because the organization did not endorse candidates. Still, when King was taken to prison, Kennedy phoned Coretta to see how he might help. Coretta was pregnant with the couple's third child at the time.

John F. Kennedy's brother and campaign manager was Robert Kennedy. As a lawyer, he understood the law. It was clear that the original traffic violation was harassment. He phoned the judge and the next day King was released.

Although it might seem the Kennedys were kind to help King, they also had their reasons. John F. Kennedy was behind Richard Nixon in the race to become president. His help in getting King released made black voters vote for him. He went on to win the election the next month and became president.

THE FREEDOM RIDERS

By 1961, African Americans, and in particular black college students and the white students that sympathized with them, were getting impatient. Despite the Supreme Court ruling that segregation on buses as well as all other transport was unconstitutional, in the South, buses still had black and white sections. The waiting rooms and lunch counters in stations were also still segregated.

In early 1961, James Farmer, the head of a civil rights group called CORE, standing for Congress of Racial Equality, started to organize what was to be called Freedom Rides.

The plan was that when colleges closed for summer vacation, college students would get on buses heading south and participate in nonviolent resistance against the stubborn segregation that the South refused to correct. They would begin in the North and travel to the Deep South traversing through many states on their way.

The first group of Freedom Riders was made up of thirteen students: a mixed group of black and white and men and women. They set off on two buses from Washington, D.C. In North and South Carolina, they encountered people who shouted rude things at them but mostly there was little violence.

When they got to Atlanta, the Freedom Riders had dinner with Dr. King. He was happy that they were using nonviolence resistance to protest against segregation, but King was afraid for them. He knew the Deep South, states like Alabama and Georgia. He advised them not to continue. He had heard rumors that the KKK was waiting for the Freedom Riders. The students listened to his advice but chose to continue.

When the buses arrived in Anniston, Alabama it was as King had said, an angry mob of white people, mostly KKK, were waiting for them at the bus terminal. They beat the students and slashed at the buses' tires.

The two buses managed to get out of the terminal. The front bus continued, but more than thirty vehicles followed the bus at the back. The bus tire became flat and they were forced to stop. One of the people in the mob threw a firebomb into the bus and then others held the door closed. Luckily, the Freedom Riders managed to get out, but the bus was burned completely. This was only one of the attacks the Freedom Riders had to endure that summer.

Despite the vicious attacks, the Freedom Riders continued to ride the buses. Between May and November of 1961, there were 60 Freedom Rides. In total, 436 students participated in the rides that summer.

THE NIGHT OF MAY 21ST, 1961

The violence the Freedom Riders faced received national coverage and soon people everywhere knew the lengths to which whites in the South would go to keep their racist segregation in place.

On Sunday May 21st, 1961, Reverend Ralph Abernathy organized a special meeting at his church in Montgomery, Alabama, the first Baptist Church. King was on a speaking tour but left and attended the meeting in Montgomery. The meeting was made up of hymns and speeches in support of the Freedom Riders. In attendance were prominent civil rights activists and some of the leaders of the Freedom Riders.

When the meeting started, a white mob arrived outside of the church. The mob grew as the evening progressed. They shouted hateful things, threw rocks at the church's windows, and lit fires. The local police arrived but soon the crowd overwhelmed them.

At the meeting, King blamed the violence that the Freedom Riders faced on the governor of Alabama, Governor Patterson.

"We hear the familiar cry that morals cannot be legislated. This may be true, but behavior can be regulated," King said. *"The law may not be able make a man love me, but it can keep him from lynching me."*

According to journalists who were there that night, the mob outside grew to more than 200 people. The civil rights activists inside of the church were being held captive. At 3 a.m., King phoned the U.S. Attorney General, Robert Kennedy. Kennedy immediately began to put pressure on Governor Patterson to do something. Eventually, the governor called for marshal law and sent in the Alabama National Guard. At dawn, the people in the church were driven out in military vehicles and escorted to safety.

Despite the hatred and violence directed at them, the Freedom Rides continued. In November 1961, the Interstate Commerce Committee, the ones who regulated state-to-state transport, banned all segregation on any sort of interstate travel.

THE FAILED ALBANY MOVEMENT

Albany, Georgia was a town where 40% of the population was black. Despite that, by October 1961, it was still as if the town and many of its people were living in a time capsule. While other parts of the South were fighting to end segregation, Albany was firmly stuck in Jim Crow laws that kept blacks and whites apart and made sure blacks could not register to vote.

In the fall of 1961, three college students from the Student Nonviolent Coordinating Committee (SNCC) arrived in Albany in the hopes of mobilizing the citizens of the town and southwestern Georgia.

Meetings were held and various protests took place with the movement gaining momentum. The NAACP joined the SNCC and eventually they decided to invite King and the SCLC to join them as well. Some SNCC members were not happy to have King involved. They felt that he had not participated in the Freedom Rides fully. At the time, King made it clear that he could not get on the buses because he was still on parole.

Still, King went to Albany and was immediately arrested in a mass arrest by the Chief of Police, Laurie Pritchett. Pritchett and the city officials had decided that they would arrest all protestors, charging them with disturbing the peace, but they would use no violence. He had learned from other cities in the South that violence caused national media attention and Albany did not want that.

King refused to pay the fine and said he would stay in jail until the city gave into their demands. The city agreed and King left Albany. Once he was gone, the government officials ignored everything they agreed to. King went back two more times, and, in both cases, he was arrested. The second time he again refused to pay the fine and Pritchett had it paid for him. King said that he'd seen protestors thrown out of a lot of places, but he'd never seen a protestor thrown out of jail.

By the summer of 1962, the groups in the Albany Movement were frustrated because they had no results even though they'd held many protests. Discipline fell apart and some demonstrations turned violent.

King saw it as a failure but learned an important lesson. It was important to focus on one aspect of segregation and try to get results. In the Albany Movement, they were trying to tackle segregation on many fronts as well as dealing with voter registration. It was too broad and had led to failure in his eyes.

DID YOU KNOW?

- Reverend Ralph Abernathy was a friend and mentor to Martin Luther King, Jr. They were founders of both MIA and SCLC and worked together on many protests including the Montgomery Bus Boycott.

- During the Freedom Rides, protestors decided to fill the jails and accepted no bail in Jackson, Mississippi. In the end, 328 of the protestors were taken to Parchman Prison, some kept on death row.

- The spring after the end of The Albany Movement, the city council removed all segregation laws from their books.

- King felt that the untouchables in India were in a similar position as African Americans in the U.S. Untouchables are the lowest caste in India's caste system and suffer from 2,000 years of oppression.

- The NAACP preferred using the courts to rid the country of segregation while SCLC preferred nonviolent resistance. Sometimes this caused problems between the two groups.

"BOMBINGTON" ALABAMA

Before 1963, Birmingham, Alabama was one of the most segregated cities in America, legally by city laws and also culturally. The population was about 60% white and 40% black and yet only 10% of the black residents had managed to register to vote.

Not a single black person was employed as a police officer or a firefighter. Blacks could not have jobs as salesclerks or cashiers; they could not be employed as bank tellers or bus drivers. No black person could be a secretary for a white professional. Blacks were nearly entirely employed in manual labor. Even when they were able to get better jobs, for example at steel mills, they received a fraction of the pay of a white person doing the same job.

Segregation in bus terminals, at lunch counters, in restrooms, and public spaces was rigidly enforced.

The pastor for the Bethel Baptist Church, civil rights activist Fred Shuttlesworth, sued the city, demanding that the parks be open to blacks. He won the case, but instead of opening the parks for use by blacks and whites, the city decided to close all of the parks.

A lot of the problem was caused by the long-time city commissioner, Eugene "Bull" Connor. Connor was a committed racist and segregationist. One example of the way he ran Birmingham was shown when the first Freedom Riders arrived in Birmingham on May 14th, 1961. Connor knew that white KKK members were waiting at the bus terminal to beat the Freedom Riders. He instructed the police under his charge to wait fifteen minutes after the buses arrived, before going to the bus terminal. This would give the KKK members time to beat the protestors.

Opposition to black civil rights was so strong that between 1945-1962 there were fifty unsolved bombings of property belonging to civil rights activists, many of them black churches. This caused Birmingham to be nicknamed Bombingham and Bombington.

Shuttlesworth had been fighting Connor and the segregationists for years with little success. He decided in 1963 he needed help and he called on Dr. King and the SCLC.

KING COMES TO BIRMINGHAM

On April 2nd, 1963, King and other leaders in the SLCL arrived in Birmingham to help Reverend Shuttlesworth. King was still stinging from his failure in Albany, so he wanted the goals for the protests in Birmingham to be truly clear. They decided that they would focus their protests on the downtown shopping area and the government district.

They had clear sets of demands

- The desegregation of downtown

- Fair hiring

- City employment of blacks

- Establishment of a bi-racial committee to oversee the desegregation of Birmingham schools

The plan was to use nonviolent protests to create a crisis that forced government officials and business leaders to negotiate with civil rights leaders.

They began by asking black residents to boycott all shops downtown. Easter was a busy time, but in April 1963, shop owners saw their sales drop. For six weeks black protestors monitored the downtown area to make sure blacks were not shopping there.

Some business owners tried to comply with what protestors wanted by taking down Jim Crow signs that read *"Colored"* and *"White."* When they did, Connor told them that if they did not follow the city's segregation laws, they would have their business licenses taken back.

Wyatt Tee Walker and the founder of SCLC came up with Project C, C standing for confrontation. He knew Connor and knew that any protests would be met with violence. Violence caused national attention, which was good for the protestors. Such code names were extensively used because the activists knew that their phones were tapped.

Project C included the boycott of downtown stores and also regular marches from the church to downtown, with protestors doing sit-ins at whites-only libraries, lunch counters, churches, and all other segregated places. Protestors would then walk to the mayor's office downtown. King promised that the marches would be daily. The plan was to fill Birmingham's jail with arrested protestors.

BIRMINGHAM, GOOD FRIDAY, 1963

Connor, knowing that Reverend Shuttlesworth and King were planning to launch a series of daily protest marches, managed to get the court to issue an injunction or a ban that made the marches illegal. In the past, King and the SLCL did not violate such injunctions but the failure in Albany made King re-think that strategy. They decided that they would march on Good Friday, April 12th, 1963.

A group of fifty was organized, including King, Abernathy, and fifty other protestors ranging in age from 15 to 80. The group was arrested along the way and charged with violating the injunction not to march. This would be King's thirteenth arrest.

The police put King in jail and for a while no one knew where he was. Only after 24 hours was he allowed to talk to the SCLC lawyer. Coretta was home in Atlanta, having just given birth to their fourth child. President Kennedy phoned her to find out how she was and to assure her they would find her husband and organize a phone call. Shortly after her husband phoned and they had a short, careful conversation knowing that their phone was being listened to by others.

King's arrest received national attention and the focus turned to Birmingham. In his jail cell he wrote the essay *"Letter from Birmingham Jail."* He was released from jail on April 20th. He was now more determined than ever to win in Birmingham.

LETTER FROM BIRMINGHAM JAIL

Dr. King and his methods of nonviolent protest were not always popular in the black community, and there was also criticism from the church. In Birmingham, some blacks saw King and SCLC as outsiders coming into the city to cause trouble and to take over the protests.

After being arrested on Good Friday, King, who was now in jail, had time to think about his many opponents that were on his own side. He began to write down what he was thinking, first in the margins of a newspaper and later on scraps of paper given to him by the Birmingham jail's janitor.

In this now famous essay, King defended his tactics from all angles, especially in regard to what they were intending to do in Birmingham.

There were many in the civil rights movement who believed that segregation was best addressed through the courts. King defended his policy of nonviolent protest. He explained how nowhere does an oppressor willingly hand freedom to the oppressed. Court rulings such as Brown vs Board of Education did not desegregate schools in Birmingham.

The clergy had criticized him for creating more tension where there was already enough tension. In the essay, he explained that indeed increasing tension is exactly what they wanted. It was that tension that forced segregationists to negotiate.

King and the SCLC were accused by some Birmingham blacks as outsiders coming to their city to cause problems. He dismissed the idea that he could be an outsider anywhere in the United States. He also said, *"…injustice anywhere is a threat to justice everywhere… As such a person who believes in justice must fight these injustices wherever they are."*

He had been accused by some people of being too radical. In the essay, he states that he is moderate, but that when it comes to commitment to the cause to free his people, he is an extremist.

He asks the reader to ignore people and that they must be calm and complacent, and things will change. They must also ignore the hateful policies of the black nationalists.

When he left jail, he gathered the bits of papers and had a secretary type it up. The editor at New York Times Magazine wanted to see it, but in the end did not publish it. It was first published in June 1963 by Liberation and later in August by The Atlantic Monthly.

THE CHILDREN'S CRUSADE

James Bevel, SCLC Director of Direct Action, came up with a plan for the Birmingham protests while King was in jail. It was named the Children's Crusade by Newsweek Magazine. They were failing to get enough black adult protestors and he decided to recruit children, children from elementary school to college age.

The thought was that since they intended not to accept bail when Connor and his police arrested them, many adults could not stay in jail since it caused them and their family much hardship. They could not work and earn a living if they were in jail. Children did not have that problem.

The SCLC trained the children and young people in the tactics of nonviolent resistance. On May 2nd, 1963, the children participated in their first march. It was from the church to downtown, stopping along the way at segregated places to do sit-ins. They marched in a disciplined manner, singing and clapping along the way. Throughout the campaign, in Birmingham, the children stuck to their nonviolent training.

On that day 600 young people were arrested. The youngest was Audrey Faye Hendricks who was nine years old.

The use of children was heavily criticized, including by Malcom X, who said that real men don't send children to fight on their behalf. Wyatt Tee Walker responded by saying that the arrested children would learn more in five days in jail than they would learn in five months in a segregated school.

At the end of that day, Birmingham Jail had 1,200 protestors being housed in a jail meant for 900. Connor was furious.

The next day, May 3rd, when the next group of young people began their march, Connor ordered that they be sprayed with high-pressure fire hoses. The hoses tore boys' shirts off and tossed people around, making them fall down in the street. Connor also used police dogs on the protestors. Journalists took photos, which were published nationally, and people were shocked and furious with the Birmingham police and firefighters under Connor's command.

Blacks in Birmingham were also angry and now even those who had opposed King began to take his side. It was the turning point in the Birmingham protests.

THE RESULTS FROM BIRMINGHAM

As May 1963 progressed, the pressure on Birmingham by the federal government and the public of the country was heavy. What people watched on TV and read in the newspapers about how the Birmingham police had treated Dr. King and the other protestors was too much. Civil rights and desegregation had taken a front seat in national discussions.

Unfortunately, there was also violence. The Gaston Hotel where King and other SCLC leaders had been staying was bombed. When police arrived to investigate, black bystanders threw items at them. It turned into a riot. Cars and buildings were burned, and people were stabbed, including a police officer. King's brother's house was also bombed. State troopers and federal soldiers were brought in to restore order.

Despite this, there was progress. On May 10th, King and Shuttlesworth held a press conference where they listed the results of negotiations with business leaders and the government.

They included:

- The desegregation of downtown lunch counters, restrooms, drinking fountains, and fitting rooms within 90 days.

- The hiring of blacks in stores as clerks and sales staff.

- The release of those in jail.

On May 21st, Bull Connor left office. Later in June all Jim Crow signs written *"Colored"* or *"Whites"* were removed from the city. In July, not all lunch counters were desegregated, but many were. No blacks had yet been hired as police officers or firefighters and still, no black lawyer could be given permission to work in Birmingham. But city parks and golf courses were open for both blacks and whites and most segregation laws were removed from the law books. The situation had improved quite a bit.

King was considered a hero to many after the campaign in Birmingham. In general, the protests in Birmingham were considered a big success.

SECOND QUIZ TIME!

1. In which city was the Prayer Pilgrimage held?

   a. Washington, D.C.
   b. Montgomery
   c. Birmingham

2. What was the main objective of the Civil Rights Act of 1957?

   a. To desegregate schools
   b. To protect African Americans' right to vote.
   c. To desegregate buses

3. What did the Supreme Court ruling in the case Brown vs the Board of Education outlaw?

   a. Segregated schools
   b. Literacy tests for voters wanting to register to vote
   c. Blacks being forced to sit at the back of the bus

4. What is the name of the woman who refused to give up her seat on the bus to a white person, an act that started the Montgomery Bus Boycott?

5. What were the Freedom Riders protesting?

   a. Blacks not being able to register to vote
   b. Segregated libraries
   c. Segregated transportation (busses, trains, planes) that travelled between states

6. Which protest campaign did Martin Luther King, Jr. think had been a failure?

INTERESTING QUOTES

The function of education is to teach one to think intensively and to think critically. Intelligence plus character - that is the goal of true education.

Martin Luther King, Jr.

Ask not what your country can do for you, but what you can do for your country.

John F. Kennedy

The best thing we can do is be a servant of God. It does good to stand up and serve others. You have to be prepared to die before you can begin to live.

Reverend Shuttlesworth

DETROIT'S WALK TO FREEDOM

Shortly after the success in Birmingham, Dr. King was asked to go to Detroit Michigan and march with the protestors to commemorate the 20th anniversary of the Detroit Race Riots of 1943. In those riots that lasted over a period of days, 34 people were killed, and hundreds injured.

The Walk to Freedom took place on June 23rd, 1963. The march itself lasted only about an hour and a half, but the marchers continued on to Cobo Arena and Hall where prominent civil rights activists gave speeches. King was among them. 125,000 people marched that day; at the time that was the largest civil rights protest in the country's history. King said it was one of the most wonderful days in the history of America.

Besides commemorating the 1943 riots, organizers of the march also wanted to protest the terrible treatment activists in the South had received by the police when fighting for their civil rights, including being sprayed with fire hoses and attacked by police dogs. Racism in the North often seemed milder than that in the South, but African Americans still faced much racism. There was inequality in hiring practices, wages, education, and housing. The Walk to Freedom wanted to highlight those issues. The last objective of the Walk was to educate people about the SCLC and to raise funds for the organization.

Reverend Clarence L. Franklin and Reverend Albert Cleage were the main organizers of the event. In the beginning, there were some problems because Cleage wanted the Walk to be for African Americans only. The NAACP said that they would not support the Walk if that was the case and the idea was forgotten.

Dr. King's speech was a version of his *"I Have A Dream"* speech that he would give in a few months' time in Washington, D.C. Motown Records asked King if they could record his speech in Detroit. He gave them permission but said that any money he might have earned on the recording should instead be donated to the SCLC.

THE MARCH ON WASHINGTON

On August 28th, 1963, one of the biggest protest marches in the history of the United States took place in Washington, D.C. It was named The March on Washington for Jobs and Freedom. Between 200,000-300,000 people marched that day with more than 75% of the marchers being African American.

At first the march was meant to be about jobs and economic equality for African Americans. African Americans faced unfair practices when looking for a job and there were many jobs they were not allowed to do. In other cases, blacks and whites doing the exact same job were paid different amounts. The black person would earn far less. The majority of African Americans were left to do only manual labor jobs.

The first organizers pulled in various groups around the country including Dr. King's SCLC and soon the objective of the march was expanded to include not just the economic rights of African Americans but also their civil rights.

Because it was such a big group of different organizations, each with their own goals, there were disagreements. Some of the organizers wanted to have civil disobedience actions along the way. For example, taking over offices in the Justice Department. Others wanted the march to be extremely critical of President Kennedy's administration and their lack of action on civil rights. Others didn't want to make the president angry. Some prominent people criticized the march completely. For example, Malcolm X called it a picnic and did not attend.

In the end, the organizers agreed on a list of objectives. The main objectives of the march were:

1. The passage of a new meaningful Civil Rights Act.

2. A public work and training program for the unemployed.

3. The passage of a Federal Fair Employment Practices Act that stopped discrimination against African Americans.

4. A federal law to stop discrimination against blacks in both public and private housing.

The march commenced from the Washington Monument ending at the Lincoln Memorial. At the Lincoln Memorial, the massive crowd listened to speeches. The last speech was Dr. King's famous *"I Have a Dream"* speech.

Many believe that the March on Washington pushed the Kennedy Administration to move on passing the Civil Rights Act of 1964.

I HAVE A DREAM

Martin Luther King, Jr.'s *"I Have a Dream"* speech is one of the most important speeches in the history of America as well as throughout the world. In 1999, a vote was taken amongst academics and they declared this speech as the best speech of the 20th century.

Unlike other speakers on the day, Dr. King only started writing his speech the night before the March on Washington. He wrote it in the hotel where he and his staff were staying. He would write something and then discuss it with his staff and then write again. At one point, one member of his team told him not to mention dreams. The person felt that King had given such speeches many times before. So, the prepared speech had no mention of dreams at all.

He started his speech mentioning that 1963 was the 100th anniversary of the signing of The Emancipation Proclamation; the law that set all slaves free. Then he said that one hundred years later African Americans were still not free.

When he started reading in front of the Lincoln Memorial that day, he read from the prepared speech. But along the way, his friend, the Gospel singer Mahalia Jackson, shouted from the crowd *"Tell 'em about the dream, Martin!"* From that point he spoke from his heart. Many felt he spoke as if speaking in his church. One of the most remembered parts of the speech was:

"I have a dream that my four little children will one day live in a nation where they will not be judged by the color of their skin, but by the content of their character. I have a dream today!"

THE CIVIL RIGHTS ACT OF 1964

After the successful civil rights actions in Birmingham and the huge March on Washington, President Kennedy was feeling pressured to do something about the rights of African Americans that were being violated. Before his assassination in November 1963, he had already proposed a comprehensive Civil Rights Act.

When Lyndon B. Johnson became president, he made sure that Kennedy's wishes were fulfilled. He told Congress that in the session that was opening they should do more for the civil rights of African Americans than in the hundred sessions that had happened before that one. Kennedy had felt the pressure to get a meaningful Civil Rights Act passed. He knew that America would not truly be free until all of its citizens were free and that could only happen if the correct laws were in place and enforced.

Representatives in Congress from the South tried their best to stop the passage of the bill. They felt that the new act would take away state rights.

The main points of the Civil Rights Act of 1964 are:

1. The end of all segregation by race, religion, or national origin in all places: public accommodation, courthouses, parks, restaurants, theaters, sports arenas, and hotels.

2. No one can be denied service based on race.

3. No federal money can be used to fund a program that discriminates against anyone by race.

4. It banned all employment discrimination based on race, sex, color, religion, or national origin.

5. It prohibited the unequal application of requirements for voters.

6. It authorized the Office of Education to help desegregate black and white schools.

Dr. King called the new Civil Rights Act a second Emancipation for African Americans.

DR. KING WINS THE NOBEL PEACE PRIZE

On October 14th, 1964, Dr. King was in a hospital bed in Atlanta, recovering after months of a punishing schedule. Coretta phoned him; she had big news. He had been chosen to receive that year's Nobel Peace Prize. It was an incredible honor and important recognition for the work that he had been doing. At the time, he was the youngest person to ever have won the Nobel Peace Prize. He was 35 years old. He was also only the second African American to have ever been awarded the prize.

The awards ceremony was in Oslo, Norway on December 10th. King left the United States on December 4th. He made a stopover in London to give sermons at St. Paul's Cathedral and to meet with peace groups there.

At the award ceremony, King said that the prize was for all of the people who worked in the civil rights movement. He called them a *"mighty army of love."* The Chairman of the Nobel Committee said that King was the first person from the Western world to show that struggles can be won using the principles of nonviolence.

The prize money was $54,000. King gave $25,000 to the Gandhi Society for Human Rights and $12,000 to SCLS. He split the rest among the NAACP, Congress for Racial Equality, National Council of Negro Women, the National Urban League, and the Student Nonviolent Coordinating Council.

Upon returning to America he was celebrated widely. Although he had just won the Nobel Prize, he immediately returned to his tough schedule of nonviolent protests around the country.

SELMA PROTESTS

By January 1965, despite the passage of the Civil Rights Act of 1964, the state of Alabama still remained firmly racist. The state's governor, George Wallace, declared himself a segregationist and wanted whites to stay in control of everything.

Dallas County, where Selma was located, was one of the worst places in terms of segregation, black voters' rights, and civil rights. At the time, the county's population was about half black and yet only 2% of African Americans were registered to vote.

By the start of 1965, the Student Nonviolent Coordinating Committee (SNCC) had been in Selma for some months trying to register black voters. In January 1965, Dr. King and the SCLC joined them.

Many peaceful demonstrations were held around Dallas County and many protestors were arrested, including King.

On the evening of February 18th, in nearby Marion, white supremacists (people who believe whites are better than other races) had started fighting peaceful protestors. The state troopers arrived trying to calm the situation. One of the African American protestors, 26-year-old Jimmie Lee Jackson, tried to protect his mother from being beaten. He was shot by police and died a few days later in hospital.

In response to Jackson's death, the leaders of the protestors decided to march from Selma to the state capital, Montgomery, a 54-mile march. Here they would deliver a petition to Governor Wallace. Wallace told state troopers to stop the march any way they could.

On Sunday, May 7th, 600 protestors left Brown Chapel AME Church in Selma heading for Montgomery. King was not among them. He had a meeting scheduled with President Johnson and had returned to Atlanta. He and his church members were going to Selma the next day.

The marchers met no resistance as they made their way through Selma. Then they came to the Edmund Petrus Bridge over the Alabama River. When they got to the other side, they found state troopers, some on horses, as well as a group of white bystanders. The marchers were told to go back. When they didn't, the troopers attacked them.

The protestors were beaten with whips, clubs, and rubber tubing wrapped in barbed wire. They were pushed to the ground. Troopers riding horses chased them. Throughout the entire event the protestors remained nonviolent. Television cameras were there, and by that night, TV sets around the country witnessed the horror. It was called Bloody Sunday.

SUCCESS IN SELMA

Americans across the country were angered by what they saw on TV. Dr. King asked religious leaders of all races and religions to join them in Selma to protest, and they came.

Two days later, King with a much larger group, set out to march to Montgomery. Again, the state troopers were waiting for them on the bridge and told them to turn back. King had the marchers kneel in prayer. After that, they returned to Selma. Some criticized him for turning back and called him a coward, but President Johnson praised him for not increasing the tension and causing more violence.

That night, one of the religious leaders, a young minister from Massachusetts, James Reeb, was beaten to death by white supremacists. The tension in the city was remarkably high.

On March 15th, President Johnson spoke on TV. He talked about the protests in Selma, protesting to fight for a right that all Americans had and the right to vote that was being denied to African Americans in Alabama. He told the American public that the protesters' cause was a cause that as Americans, everyone needed to be behind.

The protestors got a federal court order allowing them to march. President Johnson provided federal troops to protect the protestors. On March 21st, King and 2,000 marchers set off from Selma. They reached Montgomery four days later. Governor Wallace refused to meet with the protestors, but there were 50,000 supporters waiting for them when they got there.

In response to the Selma protests, President Johnson signed the Voters Right Act of 1965 that banned literacy tests as a requirement to register to vote. In places where less than 50% of the black citizens failed to register, the federal government could investigate and take over the registration process.

CHICAGO FREEDOM MOVEMENT

After Selma, Dr. King decided to broaden his attention from the South to the North. The racism in the North was just as unjust and showed King that even if laws blocking African Americans from freedom were removed, racist policies could still stay in place.

In the North, blacks were denied good housing. They were often forced to live in broken-down buildings in neighborhoods with no services. These areas were often dangerous and full of gangs. Blacks who tried to move to better neighborhoods, usually white ones, were denied loans from the banks.

In January of 1965, King and Coretta moved to the West Side of Chicago to a place called North Lawndale. King wanted to help a group that was working on the conditions for blacks in Chicago. They were called the Chicago Freedom Movement. King's two-bedroom apartment was a mess until the landlord found out that he had a famous tenant. Only then did he do repairs; however, it was still unbelievably bad.

That summer, the SCLC and the Chicago Freedom Movement held many marches and protests to try to get the city to improve conditions. The race tensions were high and in July 1966, Chicago's West Side erupted in race riots.

On the 5th of August, the two groups marched through an all-white neighborhood to protest the housing situation of African Americans. People threw bottles, stones, and bricks at the protestors and King was hit in the head with a stone. The protest was shown on TV and the country's sympathy and support turned toward King.

Mayor Daley of Chicago wanted the protests and violence to end in his city. He met with the protestors and agreed to improve things. He agreed to make the buildings used by public housing only a certain height, not the tall high-rise tenement building most blacks lived in. He also got an agreement from the Mortgage Bankers Association to make mortgages available to people no matter what their race was.

The campaign in Chicago had limited success. The mayor went back on his promises and nothing had improved by 1967. SCLC members stayed in the city and continued working on the housing programs that they had started. One of them saw people living in dilapidated buildings, forming trusts, and paying their rent money to the trust instead of the landlord. They then used that money to fix the building. The SCLC members also stayed to help continue the voter registration program.

Many feel, though, that the Fair Housing Act passed two years later was a direct result of King's protests during the summer of 1966, which shed a national light on the problems for blacks in the North.

MARCH AGAINST FEAR

James Howard Meredith was already known in the civil rights community when he began his solo March Against Fear. Meredith had been the first black student admitted to the University of Mississippi. They had admitted him without knowing he was black. When he arrived at school, they refused to allow him to start. He had to take the case to the federal court to finally take up his place at the university.

Meredith was growing tired of the slow pace at which the civil rights of African Americans were changing in the Deep South, even though there were good laws in place. Still, blacks in Tennessee and Mississippi lived nearly the same life they had lived under the Jim Crow laws and yet it was 1966. He felt he needed to do something.

He decided to take a solo march from Memphis Tennessee to Jackson Mississippi, a distance of 220 miles. His objective was to show that a black man could walk with dignity and shouldn't have to walk with fear. He also wanted to get as many African Americans along the way to register to vote. He didn't, however, want a lot of media attention or for any of the big civil rights organizations to get involved.

He set out on his walk on June 5th, 1966. On June 6th, a white man shot him while he was walking on Highway 51 in Mississippi. He was shot with birdshot, so had many wounds but none too serious. But still, he could not continue the walk. Leaders from the big civil rights organizations decided to finish the walk for Meredith, including King.

The group, by then numbering 15,000, arrived in Jackson on June 26th. Meredith joined the march again the day before. He arrived walking at the front with King and other leaders. The group included many ordinary Southerners, both black and white, who wanted change.

Along the way, the activists managed to help 4,000 African Americans to register to vote.

DR. KING OPPOSES THE VIETNAM WAR

At first, Dr. King was careful around the issue of the Vietnam War and the call for it to end by the growing Peace Movement. Since the presidency of John F. Kennedy, resources were being used for the war more and more each year. King's main reason for being careful was that he did not want to offend President Johnson since Johnson was a strong supporter of civil rights for African Americans and had done a lot for the movement. But, eventually, King's conscience gave him no choice.

When he finally made public statements about the war in Vietnam, he made it clear that he was speaking in his own capacity and not as the president of the SCLC. Many leaders in the civil rights movement opposed King expanding his area of focus. They felt that he would weaken the civil rights movement in this way.

King was beginning to see how peace and the civil rights of African Americans were linked. The massive spending on the war took away from programs targeted at the poor and blacks. He also found it ironic that young black men were travelling 8,000 miles to fight for the freedom and rights of the Vietnamese people on behalf of America while America did not give those same men those rights in their own country.

While Dr. King had to take a measured approach to fighting the war, Coretta did not. She was far more public about her opposition to the war and spoke at a large anti-war rally at the Washington Memorial on November 27th, 1965.

By 1968, King was convinced that the three most urgent problems facing America were racism, poverty, and the Vietnam War. On March 3rd, 1968, he said that he thought that the war in Vietnam might be the most unjust war ever fought in the history of the world.

His position on the war made him quite unpopular with the media, Congress, and the public.

THE SANITATION WORKERS' STRIKE IN TENNESSEE

On February 1st, 1968, two African American sanitation workers in Memphis Tennessee were crushed to death by a faulty garbage crusher in one of the city's trucks. This followed years of poor wages, dangerous working conditions, and unpaid overtime. The sanitation workers, almost all black, waited for eleven days to see what the city would do in response to these deaths. Nothing happened.

On Sunday February 11th, the workers met and decided that they were fed up. They would begin a strike the next day. On Monday they marched to City Hall to deliver their demands to the mayor, Henry Loeb. Instead, they were met by 40-50 police who led them to a nearby stadium where Henry Loeb told them to go back to work. The gathering laughed and booed at him.

By February 15th, piles of garbage were appearing around the city and the mayor hired white strikebreakers to do the job. These workers were accompanied by police but still occasionally violence flared between the strikers and the strike breakers.

King first visited Memphis to support the strikers on March 18th. He spoke to the 25,000 workers and supporters at the Mason Temple. He also met with his longtime friend, Reverend James Lawson. Lawson lived in Memphis and had been supporting the strikers since the beginning.

King left Memphis but returned again on March 28th for a planned march. He arrived late and found a massive unruly crowd. He joined Lawson at the front to lead the group. On the way, the protestors became violent, breaking windows. The march was called off but by then the police had arrived. The protestors were chased into Clayborn Hall and tear gas was thrown in. Police clubbed protestors who were lying on the ground trying to get fresh air. During the violence, police used a shotgun to kill a 16-year-old boy. His name was Larry Payne.

After the violence and the conflict between members leading the strike in Memphis, King considered not returning. But he felt he needed to go back and help bring back the idea of nonviolent resistance. He knew the strike would not be successful if it once again fell into violence.

A weary Dr. King returned to Memphis on April 3rd to speak to a group of strikers. That night he delivered his famous speech *"I've Been to the Mountaintop."*

I'VE BEEN TO THE MOUNTAINTOP

Members of the SCLC did not want Dr. King to return to Memphis. The violence on March 28th was not started by strikers who were committed to nonviolence, but by a faction of black nationalists. His friends were not sure that violence would not take place again.

But King felt obligated to return to Memphis. He needed to help the strikers restore nonviolence to the strike.

When he arrived in Memphis, he was exhausted and sick. He had a sore throat and thought he would not be up to speaking after all. He asked his friend and SCLC vice president, Ralph Abernathy, to speak on his behalf. Abernathy agreed and went to the Mason Temple, leaving King back at the hotel.

At the Mason Temple, Abernathy found that the crowd was quite disappointed that King would not be speaking. He called King at the hotel and convinced him to come to the hall and give a speech. King agreed. That night, he spoke from his heart and not from a prepared speech.

The speech, now called *"I've Been to the Mountaintop,"* was mostly about the sanitation workers' strike. He talked about the various actions that he had been involved in, such as the Montgomery Bus Boycott, the Selma March for Voters' Rights, and even the Albany Movement.

He suggested the strikers might think of boycotting white owned businesses and the products and services of white owned companies. He said that a single black person was poor, but together they were an economic powerhouse. They needed to use that power.

Towards the end of the speech, King spoke about his near-death stabbing in 1958 and how he'd like to live a long life, but he was not afraid to die. It was as if he was predicting his own death. He said:

> *"But it really doesn't matter to me now, because I've been to the mountaintop. And I don't mind. …But I'm not concerned about that now. I just want to do God's will. And He's allowed me to go up to the mountain. And I've looked over. And I've seen the Promised Land. I may not get there with you. But I want you to know tonight, that we, as a people, will get to the Promised Land."*

Andrew Young, James Jordan, and Abernathy, who were there that night, said that when Dr. King took his seat, he had tears in his eyes.

His speech that night would be his last because the next day he would be assassinated.

THE ASSASSINATION OF DR. KING

On the evening after the delivery of his speech, *"I've Been to the Mountaintop,"* to the striking sanitation workers in Memphis, Dr. King, his friends, and colleagues were preparing to go to dinner at Samuel "Billy" Kyles' home. It was the evening of April 4th, 1968.

The group was staying, as they normally did, at the Lorraine Motel. King was in room 306, a room he and Ralph Abernathy stayed in so often that it was nicknamed the *"King-Abernathy Suite."*

King made a comment to the musician Ben Branch, who would be performing that night at an event, to play a song King particularly liked. Those were the last words Dr. King ever spoke. He then stepped out onto the balcony to talk to some SCLS members in the parking lot. Before he could say anything, he was shot in the face and collapsed unconscious. It was 6:01 pm.

He was rushed to St. Joseph's Hospital where the doctors opened his chest and attempted to revive him. Their attempts failed and Dr. Martin Luther King, Jr. died at 7:05 pm.

At 8:20 pm, President Johnson was in a meeting planning for a trip to Hawaii to meet military leaders about the war in Vietnam. When he received the news of King's death, he cancelled his trip and instructed the FBI to begin one of the biggest investigations in its history. He phoned Coretta to give her his condolences. And then he declared April 7th, 1968 a national day of mourning, ordering all U.S. flags to be flown at half-mast.

Memphis police were alerted that immediately after the shot was heard, a man ran from a rooming house across the street from the Lorraine Hotel. After investigations, they found a package that had a rifle and binoculars inside. The fingerprints belonged to an escaped convict, James Earl Ray.

After an international manhunt, James Earl Ray was arrested at London's Heathrow Airport on June 8th, 1968. On March 10th, 1969, he pled guilty to murdering King and was sentenced to 99 years in prison. Ray died in prison.

His reason for killing King was unclear, but he had a history of supporting racists. His lawyer was J.B. Stoner, a white supremacist. Ray had worked on avowed segregationist George Wallace's presidential campaign in 1968, however, he never gave a reason for his actions. Instead, he tried for the rest of his life to take his guilty plea back.

The funeral was held at Ebenezer Church on April 9th. Over 300,000 mourners attended and followed King's coffin which was pulled by two mules through Atlanta. The eulogy was given by King's friend and mentor, the president of Morehouse College, Benjamin Mays.

DID YOU KNOW?

- President Johnson signed the Civil Rights Act of 1961 with more than seventy pens so that he could give them to people who supported the bill. Dr. King was given one of those pens.

- The head of the FBI, J. Edgar Hoover, had spies following Dr. King everywhere he went and had extensive recordings of his phone calls and conversations. He considered Dr. King to be a dangerous communist.

- When Dr. King was awarded the Nobel Peace Prize, former Birmingham City Commissioner, Bull Connor, said that the committee must have been scraping the bottom of the barrel.

- In 1971, King won a Grammy Award after his death for his spoken word album called *"Why I Oppose the War in Vietnam"*.

- After Dr. King's death, the doctor doing the autopsy said that, although King was only 39 years old, his heart was like a heart for a man of sixty years. It is suspected it was because of all of the stress from thirteen years of fighting in the civil rights movement.

THE AFTERMATH OF THE ASSASSINATION

After Dr. King's assassination, more than 100 cities around America erupted in violence. The disruptions began on April 4th, and in some cities, it took many days before the city's peace was restored.

It was sad in some ways that the death of a man like Martin Luther King, Jr., who stood for nonviolence, was answered with violence. President Johnson was not surprised at all about the riots that occurred. He asked his aides what they thought would happen. He said if you step on a man's neck for 300 years, when you lift your foot, he's going to beat you up.

The worst affected cities were Washington, D.C., Baltimore, Kansas City, and Chicago.

In Washington, D.C., on April 4th, crowds gathered. Led by civil rights activist Stokely Carmichael, they began to move around the city and politely asking businesses to close their stores in respect for King. Some did not and violence began with shop windows broken and goods looted.

The mayor and police seemed to have things under control the next morning as a clean-up began. Then Stokely Carmichael spoke at Howard University. Crowds began to gather and then moved through the city, damaging buildings, and setting them on fire. When firefighters arrived, they were pelted with stones and bottles and couldn't do their job.

The rioting lasted until April 8th when federal troops were called in. In total, 1,200 buildings were burned, 900 of those were stores. The damage was estimated at $27 million.

Similar riots took place all over the country. In many cities, people were killed and injured. For example, in Chicago, eleven people died and 500 were injured in the riots. It was the worst civil disturbance since the Civil War.

THE POOR PEOPLE'S CAMPAIGN

Although the end to segregation and the securing of the right to vote had been important successes, Dr. King had known that without economic security, blacks and all other poor people could not be full citizens. In November 1967, at a SCLC staff retreat, King had announced his plans to shift focus. He believed it was time to use the same technique of nonviolent resistance to push the government to take solid action against poverty and to shift the nation's attention to the indignity and injustice of poverty. In 1960, according to the census, between 22-33% of Americans lived below the poverty line and were defined as poor.

The SCLC had planned a march on Washington of more than 2,000 poor people for April 22nd, 1968. Groups from various backgrounds came together for the cause, including: Native Americans, Mexicans, Puerto Ricans, and the poor white communities.

King said that they would demand that the government create more jobs, provide unemployment insurance, establish a fair minimum wage, provide affordable quality housing ,and provide quality education for poor adults and their children so they could help themselves out of poverty.

The plan was to set up a camp on the mall in Washington, D.C., a tent camp that would be named Resurrection City and would remain in place until the demands of the Poor People's Campaign were met.

However, King's unexpected death on April 4th, 1968 stopped plans for the march on Washington.

On May 12th, 1968, the SCLC, now under the leadership of Ralph Abernathy, went ahead with the Washington March. On that day, Mother's Day, Coretta led thousands of women on a march through the city. The next day was the setting up and opening of Resurrection City. Although they wanted 50,000 protestors, in the end they had about 7,000.

The protest had problems though. The leaders of the various groups fought among themselves about what to do. To make things worse, there was a big storm in Washington, D.C. and the tents could not hold up against it, so many packed and went home. Robert Kennedy's assassination on June 5th also disrupted the protest.

The protests did force the government to include 200 counties in the list that would receive supplies of surplus food and federal agencies promised to hire poor people to run the programs targeting the poor. However, SCLC president Abernathy felt that the successes were too few.

MARTIN LUTHER KING, JR. DAY

The third Monday of January is now a federal holiday celebrating Martin Luther King, Jr.'s birthday, January 15th. The campaign to establish a national holiday in his honor began almost immediately after his death. Some states and cities did pass laws to make a holiday to celebrate King, however, many people felt that he deserved a national federal holiday in his name.

In 1979, U.S. Representative John Conyers and U.S. Senator Edmund Brooke introduced a bill to establish a holiday celebrating Martin Luther King, Jr. There was opposition on a few fronts. Some felt that a paid holiday would be too expensive for the government and other employers.

The other reason lawmakers refused to support the bill was that it went against tradition. Other federal holidays like, George Washington Day, celebrated people who had served in public office. King had not. They argued it was wrong to celebrate a private individual with a federal holiday. The bill failed.

The King family decided they needed people outside of government to help them get the holiday declared. One person they called on was the musician Stevie Wonder. He wrote a song called *"Happy Birthday"* to spread the word about the campaign to establish the holiday for Dr. King.

Those fighting for the bill made a petition and collected six million signatures of people who supported the establishment of the holiday. It was the largest number of people ever to sign a position in favor of an issue.

A new bill was brought to Congress. There was still opposition. One of the people opposing the bill was Senator Jesse Helms. He wondered if King was important enough to get a federal holiday. He also felt that King's opposition to the Vietnam War was unpatriotic. Then he submitted a 300-page document where he tried to prove that King was a communist. Despite his opposition, the bill passed both houses of Congress.

Ronald Reagan was president in 1983 when the bill came before him to sign. Previously he had opposed the bill, saying that it would be expensive for employers to have an additional paid holiday. But the support in Congress for the bill was too high and he had no option but to sign, which he did on November 2nd, 1983.

It took three years for the holiday to start. In 1986 most states began celebrating the day although a few were dragging their feet. By 2000, all fifty states celebrated the day.

Included in the bill was the establishment of a Martin Luther King, Jr. Federal Holiday Commission to oversee how the day was being celebrated. Coretta was made a lifetime member of the commission by President George H. W. Bush in May 1989.

THIRD QUIZ TIME!

1. Where did Martin Luther King, Jr. give his *"I Have a Dream"* speech?

   a. Washington, D.C.
   b. Memphis
   c. Montgomery

2. What is included in the Civil Rights Act of 1964?

   a. The end of literacy tests for voters to register
   b. A ban on all forms of racial discrimination in housing
   c. The end of segregation in all places based on race, religion, and national origin

3. What was the name of Alabama's governor who announced that he was a segregationist?
   a. Jesse Helms
   b. George Wallace
   c. Bull Connor

4. What is the name of the bridge in Selma where the protestors were stopped by the police?

5. In which city was Martin Luther King, Jr. hit in the head by a stone thrown by a white person?

   a. Washington, D.C.
   b. Selma
   c. Chicago

6. What is the name of the man who started the March Against Fear?

7. Why was Martin Luther King, Jr. in Memphis when he was assassinated?

   a. To support striking sanitation workers
   b. To help improve the housing for blacks
   c. To stage a sit-in at a whites-only theater

INTERESTING QUOTES

You're not to be so blind with patriotism that you can't face reality. Wrong is wrong, no matter who does it or says it.

Malcolm X

I have decided to stick with love. Hate is too great a burden to bear.

Martin Luther King, Jr.

I don't know what the future may hold, but I know who holds the future.

Ralph Abernathy

QUIZ ANSWERS

Answers: First Quiz Time!

1. b. Ebenezer Baptist Church
2. c. 300 years
3. a. Sharecropping
4. c. Boston University
5. Because of Mahatma Gandhi's commitment to use nonviolence civil disobedience to fight injustice.
6. Montgomery, Alabama

Answers: Second Quiz Time!

1. a. Washington, D.C.
2. b. To protect African Americans' right to vote.
3. a. Segregated schools
4. Rosa Parks
5. c. Segregated transportation (busses, trains, planes) that travelled between states
6. The Albany Movement

Answers: Third Quiz Time!

1. a. Washington, D.C.
2. c. The end of segregation in all places based on race, religion, and national origin
3. b. George Wallace
4. Edmund Petrus Bridge
5. c. Chicago
6. James Howard Meredith
7. a. To support striking sanitation workers

CONCLUSION

Martin Luther King, Jr. lived only 39 years but during those short years he helped to dramatically change the life of African Americans. He had a vision of fairness and justice that was noticeably clear. It was fed from his Christian beliefs and his faith in democracy. Using the principles of Mahatma Gandhi's nonviolent resistance, he showed that violence did not need to be met with violence to be defeated.

Actions he led in places such as Birmingham, Montgomery and Selma resulted in laws that changed the lives of blacks. Legislation stemmed from those actions, including the Civil Rights Act of 1957, the Civil Rights Act of 1960, the Civil Rights Act of 1965, and the Voter Rights Act of 1965.

He often referred to the Declaration of Independence and the United States Constitution to find where the treatment of African Americans did not stand up to the agreed principles that the country held so dear. He had faith in those documents, and he expected them to be respected.

He also knew how to use the media to let the entire country see what was being done in their name. He then made appeals to people across the country to their sense of morality and their consciences to ask if what was happening was acceptable. Once the people of America were on board, it was easier to get the government to follow.

Dr. King was not always the one who began a certain protest, but instead he was the one who made sure that the local organizers were able to stay on track. He let them see that what they were doing was in line with the foundations set by the founders of the country. This gave them courage that the actions they were taking, despite the often vicious opposition against them, was right and just.

Martin Luther King, Jr. was a great coalition builder. His SCLC was a coalition of religious people and civil rights activists. When he and his organization joined a local protest, he joined with the local organizers. He knew the power of working together to achieve the people's goals.

At the end of his short life, King began to see more clearly how racism, poverty, and war worked together to keep African Americans and other minorities oppressed. Sadly, because of his early death, we will never know what effects the expansion of his work could have had on the country and the people who he supported.

CPSIA information can be obtained
at www.ICGtesting.com
Printed in the USA
LVHW061358281221
707330LV00008B/366